Phonemic Awareness Activities for Early Reading Success

Easy, playful activities
that help prepare children
for phonics instruction

by Wiley Blevins

Cover design by Kathy Massaro
Cover illustration by Laura Cornell
Interior design by LDL Designs
Interior illustrations by Maxie Chambliss

ISBN 0-590-37231-9
Copyright © 1997 by Wiley Blevins
All rights reserved.
Printed in the U.S.A.

Table of Contents

Table of Contents

What Is Phonemic Awareness?

The two best predictors of early reading success are alphabet recognition and phonemic awareness. — Marilyn Jager Adams

Phonemic awareness is the understanding that words are made up of sounds. It is also the ability to pick out and manipulate sounds in spoken words. Phonemic awareness is not the same thing as phonics. Phonemic awareness deals with sounds in spoken words, whereas phonics involves the relationship between sounds and written symbols. Therefore, phonics deals with learning sound-spelling relationships and is associated with print. Most phonemic awareness tasks, however, are purely oral.

According to Marilyn Jager Adams, a researcher and author on early reading, there are five basic types of phonemic awareness tasks.

- **Task 1—The ability to hear rhymes and alliteration**

Sample exercise: Listen to a nursery rhyme. Have children identify the rhyming words heard.

- **Task 2—The ability to do oddity tasks**

Sample exercise: Look at these pictures—*sock, sun, man*. Which picture name begins with a different sound? (*man*)

- **Task 3—The ability to orally blend words and split syllables**

Sample exercise: I will say the first sound of a word and then the rest of the word. Say the word as a whole. /s/ . . . at. What's the word? (*sat*)

- **Task 4—The ability to orally segment words (including counting sounds)**

Sample exercise: What sounds do you hear in the word *sat*? (/s/ /a/ /t/)

- **Task 5—The ability to do phonemic manipulation tasks**

Sample exercise: Replace the first sound in the word *sat* with /m/. What's the new word? (*mat*)

The first four phonemic awareness task types should be covered by the end of kindergarten. The fifth task type is appropriate for introduction in middle to late first grade. Each task type does not have to be mastered before moving on to the next. Rather, a mix of appropriately sequenced activities throughout lessons keeps children engaged and provides practice with all types of phonemic awareness tasks. However, instruction in oral blending should begin before instruction in oral segmentation.

In addition to these five task types, phonemic awareness exercises include phoneme discrimination activities, which also help children to focus on specific sounds in words. For example, children might be asked to listen for vowel sounds. Since vowel sounds are necessary for decoding, and children's early temporary spellings often omit vowels, much practice is provided to help children hear and distinguish these sounds in words.

Phonics and Phonemic Awareness— What's the Difference?

Phonemic awareness is the understanding that spoken words are made up of a series of discrete sounds.

Phonics deals with the learning of sound-spelling relationships and is associated with printed words.

Why Is Phonemic Awareness Important?

Children sometimes come to school unaware that words consist of a series of discrete sounds. Phonemic awareness activities help children learn to distinguish individual sounds, or phonemes, within words. This awareness is a prerequisite skill before children can learn to associate sounds with letters and manipulate sounds to blend words (during reading) or segment words (during spelling).

Often children who have difficulties with phonics instruction do so because they have not developed the prerequisite phonemic awareness skills that many children gain through years of exposure to rhymes, songs, and being read to. Phonemic awareness training provides the foundation on which phonics instruction is built. **Thus, children need solid phonemic awareness training in order for phonics instruction to be effective.** For example, phonics instruction that begins by asking a child what sound the words *sit, sand,* and *sock* have in common will not make sense to a child who has difficulty discriminating sounds in words, cannot segment sounds within words, or does not understand what is meant by the term *sound*. Children must be able to segment and auditorily discriminate /s/ in the words *sit, sand,* and *sock* before it makes sense to them that the letter *s* stands for this sound in these written words. In addition, children must be able to segment the sounds in a word such as *sit* (/s/ /i/ /t/) in order to spell the word.

Research indicates that approximately 20 percent of children are affected by a lack of phonemic awareness. This is a sizable population. Without early preventive measures, many of these children end up being labeled learning disabled or dyslexic and continue to fall behind their peers in reading development. However, this doesn't have to be the scenario. Promising phonemic awareness training studies have revealed two important points: 1) phonemic awareness can be taught, and 2) it doesn't take significant amounts of time to bring many children's phonemic awareness abilities up to a level at which phonics instruction will begin to make sense. In fact, some studies have shown results in as little as 11–15 hours of intensive phonemic awareness training spread out over an appropriate time period.

How Can I Teach Phonemic Awareness?

Phonemic awareness training can be used to help children:
- recognize rhyme and alliteration;
- do oddity tasks;
- orally blend word parts;
- clap syllables in words;
- count sounds in words;
- orally segment words;
- perform phonemic manipulation tasks;

- distinguish between a word and a sound;
- isolate beginning, middle, and ending sounds in words;
- auditorily discriminate specific sounds in words;
- prepare for phonics instruction.

Most phonemic awareness activities are oral. They are playful in nature and provide an engaging way for children to discriminate the sounds that make up words. For example, oral blending exercises help children to hear how sounds are put together to make words. These activities will lead to decoding, in which children begin sounding out or blending words independently. Children who have difficulty orally blending words will have difficulty blending, or sounding out, words while reading. Oral blending exercises begin with blending larger word parts, such as syllables, and progress to blending onsets and rimes, and finally whole words sound by sound. The earliest oral blending exercises use words that begin with continuous consonants, such as *s*, *m*, *l*, *f*, *r*, and *z*. These consonant sounds can be sustained without distortion. This makes it easier for children to hear the distinct sounds and more efficient to model the principle of oral blending, because all the sounds in the words can be "sung" together in a more natural manner. For example, the word *sat* can be stretched out and sung like this: *sssssssaaaaaaaaaat*. Movements can also be added to help children note when the speaker goes from one sound to the next. Many children will benefit from these visual cues.

Oral segmentation activities help children to separate words into sounds. These exercises begin with a focus on syllables, which are easier to distinguish than individual sounds. Segmentation activities will lead to spelling, in which children begin segmenting words into their component sounds in order to write them. Children who have difficulty orally segmenting words will have difficulty breaking apart words in order to spell them. You can tell if a child is developing the necessary segmentation skills when he or she begins asking questions such as "What makes the /a/ sound in *cat*?" or "What makes the /sh/ sound in *shop*?"

With the addition of oral blending and segmentation instruction, phonemic awareness training can have a significant impact on children's reading and writing development. And phonemic awareness continues to develop as phonics instruction begins. In fact, some aspects of phonemic awareness continue to develop through high school. Research shows that once a basic level of phonemic awareness is achieved and phonics instruction can be effective, children's phonics and phonemic awareness skills enjoy a reciprocal relationship, enhancing each other. In fact, the combination of blending and segmenting sounds and learning sound-spelling correspondences has proven to be very powerful.

Some Other Ideas to Keep in Mind:
- **Phonemic awareness is not related to print.** A child can possess some level of phonemic awareness before learning the alphabet. Since most phonemic awareness activities are oral, written words or letters should not be the focus of phonemic awareness activities until children can readily identify the letters of the alphabet. However, once children know the letters of the alpha-

bet, these visual cues will benefit many children. This generally happens in the second half of kindergarten. Before that, using print may distract from the purposes of the activities or cause confusion for children.

• **Although the phonemic awareness activities will provide you with evaluative information on your children's progress, avoid using the activities as assessments.** Keep the tone fun and informal. It is important that children are engaged in playing with language, not concerned about being assessed. Respond favorably and enthusiastically to their attempts.

• **In small groups all children can participate in and enjoy the language play activities in this book.** However, children will progress through the phonemic awareness activities at varying rates. Some children will catch on quickly; others will not. Continue to informally monitor children throughout the year. Watch for patterns of difficulty over time.

• **Model, model, model!** Continually model for children how to accomplish the various phonemic awareness tasks. In addition, provide corrective feedback. Much of the learning will occur through this feedback.

• **Most poor readers have weak phonological sensitivity (phonemic awareness skills).** This may stand in their way of learning to read and write. Therefore, phonemic awareness is not an issue of importance to only primary grade teachers. Teachers at the intermediate grades should also assess their poor readers' phonemic awareness skills. Some of the difficulties these readers face might be traced back to a lack of phonological sensitivity. Therefore, these children will benefit from phonemic awareness training, too.

• **Nothing can take the place of reading, writing, and listening to stories in an early literacy program.** Therefore, whatever you do with phonemic awareness should be done in the context of a print-rich environment with multiple language experiences.

About This Book

The phonemic awareness activities in this book can be used to supplement and enhance any reading program. They are ideal for use as warm-up exercises before phonics or other language arts instruction.

Most of the activities in the book can be used for instructional purposes. However, the games and activity pages are not intended for the initial introduction or instruction of skills. Rather, they are intended for practice and review.

Training Programs

Children with weak phonemic awareness skills will benefit from a complete phonemic awareness training program. Here is a handful of phonemic awareness training programs that are commercially available:

Auditory Discrimination in Depth: Developed by C.H. Lindamood and P.C. Lindamood. 1984. Allen, TX. DLM/Teaching Resources Corporation.

Phonological Awareness Training for Reading: Developed by Joseph K. Torgesen and Brian R. Bryant. 1994. Austin, TX. PROD-ED, Inc.

Scholastic Phonemic Awareness Kit: Written by Wiley Blevins. Program Consultants: Louisa Cook Moats and John Shefelbine. 1997. New York, NY. Scholastic Inc.

Sound Foundations: Developed by B. Byrne and R. Fielding-Barnsley. 1991. Artarmon, New South Wales, Australia. Leyden Educational Publishers.

Assessment

To determine children's phonemic awareness abilities, give one of the following commercially available assessments:

Lindamood Auditory Conceptualization Test. (Lindamood and Lindamood, 1979). Hingham, MA: Teaching Resources Corporation.

Test of Auditory Analysis Skills in *Helping Children Overcome Learning Difficulties* (Rosner, 1979). New York, Walker.

Test of Phonological Awareness, or **TOPA** (Torgeson and Bryant, 1994). Austin, TX: Pro-Ed.

Scholastic Phonemic Awareness Assessment available in the Scholastic *Phonemic Awareness Kit,* Scholastic, 1997.

Yopp-Singer Test of Phonemic Awareness in "A Test for Assessing Phonemic Awareness in Young Children" (Yopp, 1995), *The Reading Teacher,* 49 (1), pp. 20–29.

If these tests are not available, you can use select activities from this book to individually assess each child. These activities cover each type of phonemic awareness task found in most commercially available assessments.

Activity 10: oddity task

Activity 15: oral blending

Activity 35: oral segmentation

Begin assessment in midyear kindergarten and continue to assess at the beginning of grades 1–5.

Scope and Sequence

Phonemic awareness instruction should be explicit and logically sequenced. The following chart represents a suggested scope and sequence for twenty weeks of instruction. The scope and sequence is designed for the second semester of kindergarten, but can be modified for grades 1 and 2. See the Skill List that follows for a suggested sequence within each skill category.

SKILL	SCOPE AND SEQUENCE • = 1 week																			
	WEEK 1	WEEK 2	WEEK 3	WEEK 4	WEEK 5	WEEK 6	WEEK 7	WEEK 8	WEEK 9	WEEK 10	WEEK 11	WEEK 12	WEEK 13	WEEK 14	WEEK 15	WEEK 16	WEEK 17	WEEK 18	WEEK 19	WEEK 20
1. Rhyme/Alliteration	•	•	•	•	•	•	•	•	•	•										
2. Oddity Tasks		•	•	•	•	•	•	•	•	•	•	•								
3. Oral Blending			•	•	•	•	•	•	•	•	•	•	•	•	•	•	•	•	•	•
4. Oral Segmentation									•	•	•	•	•	•	•	•	•	•	•	•
5. Phonemic Manipulation																	•	•	•	•
6. Linking Sounds to Spellings																			•	•

Teaching the Skills: A Suggested Sequence

1. RHYME/ALLITERATION
a. rhyme
Example: I once saw a <u>cat</u> sitting next to a <u>dog</u>. I once saw a <u>bat</u> sitting next to a <u>frog</u>.
b. alliteration
Example: <u>S</u>ix <u>s</u>nakes <u>s</u>ell <u>s</u>odas and <u>s</u>nacks.
c. assonance
Example: The l<u>ea</u>f, the b<u>ea</u>n, the p<u>ea</u>ch—all were within r<u>ea</u>ch.

2. ODDITY TASKS
a. rhyme
Example: Which word does not rhyme: *cat, sat, pig?* (pig)
b. beginning consonants
Example: Which two words begin with the same sound: *man, sat, sick?* (sat, sick)
c. ending consonants
Example: Which two words end with the same sound: *man, sat, ten?* (man, ten)
d. medial sounds (long vowels)

Example: Which word does not have the same middle sound: *take, late, feet?* (feet)
  e. medial sounds (short vowels)
    Example: Which two words have the same middle sound: *top, cat, pan?* (can, pan)
  f. medial sounds (consonants)
    Example: Which two words have the same middle sound: *kitten, missing, lesson?* (missing, lesson)

3. ORAL BLENDING
  a. syllables
    Example: Listen to the word parts. Say the word as a whole. ta . . . ble—What's the word? (table)
  b. onset/rime
    Example: Listen to these word parts. Say the word as a whole. /p/ . . . an—What's the word? (pan)
  c. phoneme by phoneme
    Example: Listen to these word parts. Say the word as a whole. /s/ /a/ /t/—What's the word? (sat)

4. ORAL SEGMENTATION
  a. syllables
    Example: Listen to this word: *table.* Say it syllable by syllable. (ta . . . ble)
  b. onset/rime
    Example: Listen to this word: *pan.* Say the first sound in the word and then the rest of the word. (/p/ . . . an)
  c. phoneme by phoneme (counting sounds)
    Example: Listen to this word: *sat.* Say the word sound by sound. (/s/ /a/ /t/) How many sounds do you hear? (3)

5. PHONEMIC MANIPULATION
  a. initial sound substitution
    Example: Replace the first sound in *mat* with /s/. (sat)
  b. final sound substitution
    Example: Replace the last sound in *mat* with /p/. (map)
  c. vowel substitution
    Example: Replace the middle sound in *map* with /o/. (mop)
  d. syllable deletion
    Example: Say *baker* without the *ba.* (ker)
  e. initial sound deletion
    Example: Say *sun* without the /s/. (un)
  f. final sound deletion
    Example: Say *hit* without the /t/. (hi)
  g. initial phoneme in a blend deletion
    Example: Say *step* without the /s/. (tep)
  h. final phoneme in a blend deletion
    Example: Say *best* without the /t/. (bes)

ACTIVITY 1: Listen Up!

SKILL: phoneme discrimination

For this activity, you will select a specific sound for children to listen for, such as long *a*, and then read aloud a list of words. Every time children hear the target sound in a word, they are to clap their hands, repeat the sound, hold up a counter, or choose some other designated way of responding. Watch for children who are waiting for peers to respond first and then copying their responses. At a later time, you may repeat the activity with these children individually.

Sample:

Explain to children that you are going to play a listening game. They are going to listen for words with /ā/ as in *make*. You will say a word. If they hear /ā/, children are to clap their hands. If they clap their hands after a word that does not contain the sound, ask children to listen again as you repeat the word, emphasizing the vowel sound by extending it. For example, *maaaaaaaake*. Continue with these and other words: *same, rain, hope, game, late, paint, time, say.*

For subsequent *Listen Up!* exercises, use the following sequence of sounds:

- **listening for beginning consonant sounds**
  Note: Begin with continuous consonants (*f, l, m, n, r, s, v, z*) before stop consonants (*b, d, g, k, p, t*). In addition, avoid using words with blends in the early exercises. For example, use words such as *sell, sick,* and *fog* before using words such of *spell, stick,* and *frog.*

- **listening for ending consonant sounds**

- **listening for long-vowel sounds in the medial position**
  Note: Long-vowel sounds are easier for children to auditorily discriminate than short-vowel sounds. Since vowel sounds are often left out of children's early invented spellings, much work should be done listening for and discriminating these sounds.

- **listening for short vowel sounds in the medial position**

- **listening for medial consonant sounds**

SUGGESTION BOX: For children having difficulty discriminating sounds, help them to hear the sounds by saying the words slowly, extending each sound. Then point out the mouth position (lips, tongue) when making each sound. In addition, ask children whether or not they feel a burst of air or a throat vibration when making each sound. To demonstrate this, choose two highly contrasting sounds such as /g/ and /p/, or /m/ and /f/. Ask children to place their hands in front of their mouths when making each sound. Do they feel a burst of air? Ask them to place their hands on their throats when making each sound. Do they feel a vibration? Finally, ask them to explain the placement of their tongue and lips when making each sound. Are their lips open or closed?

ACTIVITY 2: Sound Match ....

SKILL: phoneme discrimination (practice page)

*S*ound Match is designed to assess children's abilities to identify pictures whose names contain the same initial, medial, or final sound. *Middle Match* (see page 14) asks children to identify pictures whose names have the same medial sound.

Using page 14 as a template and the pictures cards on pages 28 and 29, you can create the following additional activity pages:

Beginning Match (initial sounds)
- Page 1: fan, fish, leaf, lock, man, mop, six, sock
- Page 2: ball, boat, dog, duck, gate, goat, ten, top

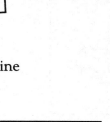

Middle Match (medial sounds)
- Page 1: gate, cake, boat, soap, feet, leaf, kite, nine
- Page 2: bat, can, fish, pig, sock, top, sun, duck

Ending Match (final sounds)
- Page 1: bat, feet, bus, glass, cake, duck, can, sun
- Page 2: coat, gate, man, ten, soap, mop, wheel, ball

> **SUGGESTION BOX:** Initial sounds are the beginning sounds in words, such as /s/ in the word *sat*. Medial sounds are the middle sounds in words, such as /a/ in the word *sat*. Medial sounds are the most difficult for children to auditorily discriminate. Do not expect early mastery of this skill. Final sounds are the ending sounds in words, such as /t/ in the word *sat*.

Middle Match

ACTIVITY 3: Higglety, Pigglety, Pop...........

SKILL: rhyme

Write the rhyme "Higglety, Pigglety, Pop" on chart paper. Read it aloud as you track the print. Reread the rhyme doing one or all of the following:

• **Have children point out the rhyming words in the poem.** Then frame the rhyming words as you reread the poem. Have children clap every time you read one of the rhyming words. In later readings, pause before the words *mop* and *flurry* to allow children to provide the rhyming words.

• **Substitute poem words.** For example, using a stick-on note, substitute the word *pop* with the nonsense word *pag*. Children will then suggest a rhyming word to replace *mop*, such as *bag* or *rag*. Write the word on a stick-on note and place it in the appropriate place in the poem. Help children to reread the new poem.

• **Have children clap the rhythm of the poem as you read it aloud.**

• **Have children substitute the syllable *la* for every syllable they hear in the poem.** The first two lines will be read *Lalala, Lalala, la; La la la lala la la.*

Higglety, Pigglety, Pop

Higglety, pigglety, pop,

The dog has eaten the mop.

The pig's in a hurry,

The cat's in a flurry,

Higglety, pigglety, pop.

SUGGESTION BOX: Explain to children that rhyming words are words that sound the same at the end, such as *pop* and *mop*. Model for children how to make a rhyme. For example, you might say, "The words *pop* and *mop* rhyme because they sound the same at the end. They both end with /op/. I can make another word that rhymes with *pop* and *mop*. This word begins with /h/ and ends with /op/. It's *hop*. Can you make a word that rhymes with *pop* and *mop*?"

Children's Books That Play with Sound

> One of the easiest and most accessible ways to improve children's sensitivity to the phonemes that make up our language is through the use of children's books that play with speech sounds through rhyme, alliteration, assonance, and phonemic manipulation. —*Griffith & Olson (1992); Yopp (1995)*

The activities used with "Higglety, Pigglety, Pop" also can be used with other poems or alliterative stories. Use classroom collections of rhymes or any trade books that spotlight rhyme and alliteration. The following is a list of books that are excellent for increasing children's awareness of rhyme and alliteration. Reread these books so children can enjoy the playful language each contains. While reading them discuss the language used. For example, you might comment on words that rhyme or a series of words that begin with the same sound. Many of the books can be extended by having children create additional rhyming verses or writing another version of the story, using rhyme or alliteration.

BOOKS WITH RHYME

Buzz Said the Bee by W. Lewison (Scholastic, 1992)

Catch a Little Fox by Fortunata (Scholastic, 1968)

Each Peach Pear Plum by Janet and Alan Ahlberg (Puffin Books, 1986)

A Giraffe and a Half by S. Silverstein (HarperCollins, 1964)

The Hungry Thing by J. Slepian and A. Seidler (Scholastic, 1988)

I Can Fly by R. Krauss (Western Publishing, 1992)

If I Had a Paka by C. Pomerantz (Mulberry, 1993) *multiple languages

Jamberry by B. Degen (HarperCollins, 1983)

Miss Mary Mack and Other Children's Street Rhymes by J. Cole & S. Calmenson (Morrouno, 1990)

101 Jump-Rope Rhymes by J. Cole (Scholastic, 1989)

Pat the Cat by C. Hawkins and J. Hawkins (G. P. Putnam's Sons, 1993)

Pickle Things by M. Brown (Parents Magazine Press/Putnam & Grosset, 1980)

The Random House Book of Poetry for Children (Random House, 1983)

See You Later Alligator by B. Strauss and H. Friedland (Price Stern, 1986)

Sheep in a Jeep by N. Shaw (Houghton Mifflin, 1986)

Sing a Song of Popcorn by B. de Regniers, B. Schenk, M. White, and J. Bennett (Scholastic, 1988)

Yours Till Banana Splits: 201 Autograph Rhymes by J. Cole and S. Calmenson (Beech Tree, 1995)

BOOKS WITH ALLITERATION

All About Arthur (an absolutely absurd ape) by E. Carle (Franklin Watts, 1974)

Alphabears by K. Hague (Henry Holt, 1984)

Animalia by G. Base, (Abrams, 1986)

Dinosaur Chase by C. Otto (HarperCollins, 1993)

Dr. Seuss's ABC by Dr. Seuss (Random House, 1963)

Faint Frogs Feeling Feverish and Other Terrifically Tantalizing Tongue Twisters by L. Obligade (Viking, 1983)

Six Sick Sheep: 101 Tongue Twisters by J. Cole and S. Calmenson (Beech Tree, 1993)

Tongue Twisters by C. Keller (Simon and Schuster, 1989)

Zoophabets by R. Tallon (Scholastic, 1979)

VIDEOS AND AUDIOCASSETTES

Clifford's Fun with Rhymes (Scholastic/Family Home Entertainment, 1992)

Jump Up and Sing: Binyah's Favorite Songs (Nick Jr./Sony Wonder, 1996)

Kidsongs®: Very Silly Songs (Warner Bros. Records, 1991)

Singable Songs for the Very Young by Raffi (Troubador Records Ltd., 1976)

SUGGESTION BOX: For additional books, see "Read-Aloud Books for Developing Phonemic Awareness: An Annotated Bibliography," by Hallie Kay Yopp in *The Reading Teacher*, Vol. 48, No. 6, March 1995.

.... ACTIVITY 4: Do You Know?

SKILL: rhyme

Write the song "Do You Know?" on chart paper. Sing it to the tune of "Muffin Man." Track the print as you sing. Sing the song several times, having children suggest one-syllable rhyming words to replace the words *king* and *ring*. Write the words on stick-on notes and place them in the appropriate places in the song.

Do You Know?

Do you know two rhyming words,
Two rhyming words,
Two rhyming words?
Oh, do you know two rhyming words?
They sound a lot alike.

<u>King</u> and <u>ring</u> are two rhyming words,
Two rhyming words,
Two rhyming words.
<u>King</u> and <u>ring</u> are two rhyming words.
They sound a lot alike.

.... ACTIVITY 5: Extend the Rhyme

SKILL: rhyme

Explain to children that you are going to say three rhyming words, such as *cat, hat,* and *sat*. You want them to listen carefully to the words and then suggest other words that rhyme. For example, children might respond with *bat, fat, mat,* and *pat*. Continue with these and other sets of rhyming words:

- tip, sip, rip
- bell, sell, well
- pan, man, van
- top, hop, stop
- bug, tug, rug

SUGGESTION BOX: After children begin learning sound-spelling correspondences, use a pocket chart and letter cards to extend this activity. After completing the exercise orally, place the common phonogram in the pocket chart. A phonogram is the part of a one-syllable word that includes the vowel and everything after it. For example, *-at* is the phonogram in the words *cat, sat,* and *hat*. A phonogram is also referred to by linguists as a *rime*. Then, one at a time, add an initial consonant to the phonogram to form a new word. Help children to blend each word formed. Point out that the words rhyme because their ending parts sound the same.

ACTIVITY 6: Make a Rhyme................................

SKILL: rhyme

Using the following incomplete poems, have children create rhymes. In each poem, children will suggest words to fill in each blank. Write the words on stick-on notes and place them in the rhyme. Then help the class to read the rhyme they created.

You can do the same activity with rhymes from your classroom collection. Write the rhyme on chart paper, replacing the second word in a rhyming pair with a blank.

TEDDY BEAR

Teddy Bear, Teddy Bear,
Jump around
Teddy Bear, Teddy Bear,
Touch the _____.
Teddy Bear, Teddy Bear,
Open the box.
Teddy Bear, Teddy Bear,
Pull out the _____.
Teddy Bear, Teddy Bear,
Bake a cake.
Teddy Bear, Teddy Bear,
Swim in the _____.

ONCE I SAW

Once I saw a cat,
And it wore a funny little _____.
Tra-la-la, La-la-la-la-la-la
Silly little cat.

Once I saw a pig,
And it wore a funny little _____.
Tra-la-la, La-la-la-la-la-la
Silly little pig.

Once I saw a goat,
And it wore a funny little _____.
Tra-la-la, La-la-la-la-la-la
Silly little goat.

ACTIVITY 7: Rhyme and Alliteration

SKILLS: rhyme and alliteration

Rename It: Have children create silly rhyming or alliterative words using names of favorite book characters. For example, *Babbit the Rabbit* or *Running Ronnie Rabbit*. Using these names, have children dictate a class story. Write the story on chart paper and reread it in subsequent days.

Silly Sentences: Help children to create silly alliterative sentences. For example, "Six snakes sell sodas." Create an alliteration book using the sentences. Have children illustrate their sentences.

Picture Rhyme: Have children fold a piece of paper in half. Ask them to draw pictures of two things whose names rhyme. For example, a *hat* and a *bat*. Help children to label the picture names. For children struggling with this activity, provide them with the name of one item to draw, such as a *star, pan, pig, pen,* or *coat*. Gather the drawings and bind them into a rhyme book for the class library.

Round Robin Rhyme: Have the children sit in a circle. Tell them that you are going on an imaginary trip. You will say one item that you want to take on the trip. The children are to repeat the item and then name another item name that rhymes. For example, if you say, "I'm going to the park and I'm taking a *mat*," the next child in the circle might say, "I'm going to the park and I'm taking a *mat* and a *hat*." Continue around the circle until no more rhyming names can be found. As a variation, you might have children state aloud items whose names begin with the same sound. For example, "I'm going to the park and I'm taking a *ball*, a *bat*, a *basket*, a *blanket*, and a *banana*."

Potpourri

Rhyme Hunt: Tell children that "we're going on a rhyme hunt," and ask them to find something in the room that rhymes with a given word. For example, what rhymes with *sock* (clock), *bear* (chair), *look* (book), *label* (table), *floor* (door), and *blue* (glue). Continue with other words and objects. You might also wish to go outside and do the activity.

Rhyme Book: Create a rhyme book. Paste a picture at the top of a page. You might wish to use the pictures on pages 28 and 29. Have children draw pictures of objects whose names rhyme or find pictures in magazines. Then gather the pictures and bind them into a class book.

Rhyme Collage: Ask children to cut out magazine pictures of objects whose names rhyme. Have them make rhyme collages with the pictures. Display the collages on a classroom bulletin board. As a variation, have children cut out magazine pictures of objects whose names begin or end with the same sound. Have them make sound collages with the pictures.

ACTIVITY 8: Rhyme Time.....

SKILL: rhyme (practice page)

Rhyme Time (page 22) is designed to provide children with practice using rhyme. It is also a way to assess their understanding of rhyme. Have children cut out the pictures at the bottom of the page. Then have them paste each picture next to the picture whose name rhymes.

You can make additional activity pages using this page as a template. The following pictures on pages 28 and 29 can be used to create the rhyming pairs: *bat/cat, bat/hat, boat/coat, can/fan, man/pan, clock/sock, frog/log, coat/goat, boat/goat, lock/clock, mop/top, cake/snake.*

Rhyme Time

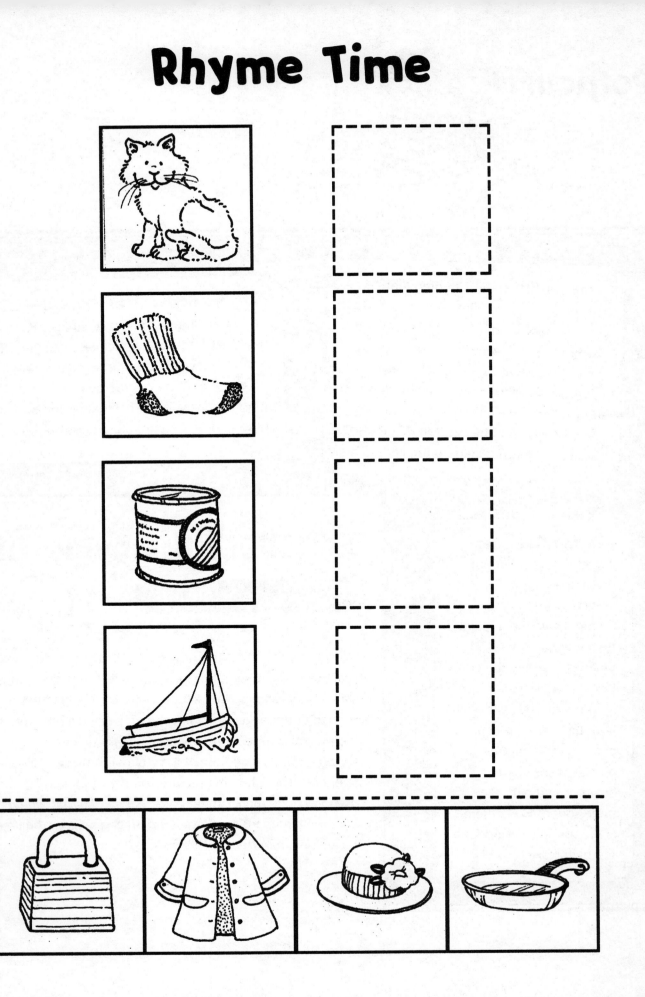

ACTIVITY 9: Mouse House ....

SKILL: rhyme (game)

Materials

game board (pages 24 and 25)
place marker for each player
number die (see page 26)

Set-Up

• Make a copy of the game board and number die. Construct the die by folding along the dotted lines and using tape to attach the die tabs to the die squares.

To Play

1. Each player chooses a place marker and puts it on START (the mouse).
2. The first player throws the die and moves his or her marker along the game board path the number of spaces on the die. (The object of the game is to help the mouse find its house.)
3. If the player lands on a picture square, he or she then states the name of the picture and a word that rhymes with the picture's name. For example, if the player lands on the picture of a pig, he or she might say pig/big. If the player is unable to state a rhyming word, he or she skips a turn. If the player lands on a piece of cheese, he or she doesn't have to say anything.
4. Each player continues in turn. The first player to reach FINISH (the mouse house) wins.

You might wish to vary the activity by replacing the picture squares with new pictures.

> **SUGGESTION BOX:** The games throughout the book are not intended to introduce a concept, rather they are designed for practice and review. The following suggestions will help you adapt the games for your class:
> 1. Enlarge game boards, game cards, and other game pieces on a photocopier, if desired.
> 2. Paste game boards onto larger pieces of colored construction paper before decorating and laminating. (When game boards are on two pages, tape the halves together.)
> 3. Paste picture cards onto colored index cards, then laminate.
> 4. Place the games in an accessible area in your classroom and encourage children to play during free time.
>
> One of the best ways to teach children how to play the games—and maximize their gains—is to model when you first use them. This can be achieved by playing for both players, playing against children while assisting them, or teaching one group of children how to play and then having them demonstrate it for their classmates.

Mouse House

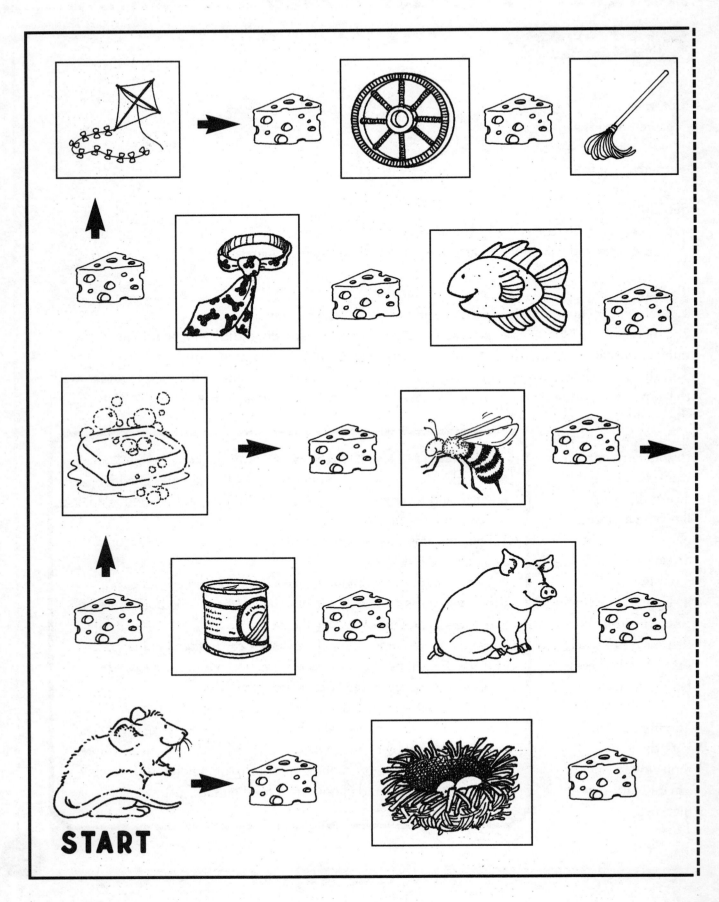

START

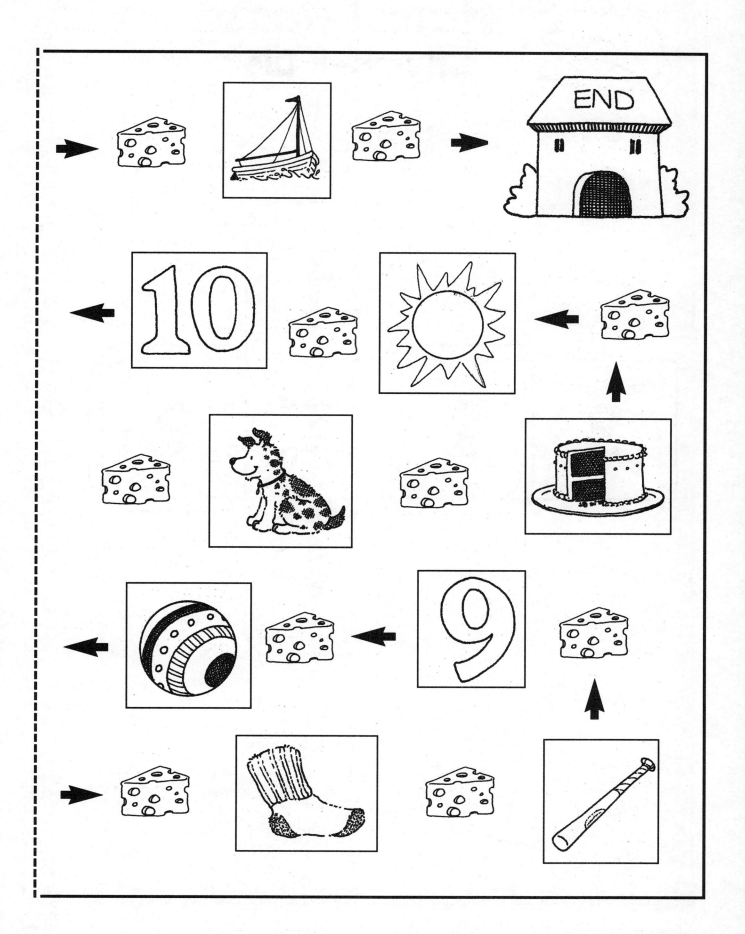

Mouse House
Number Die

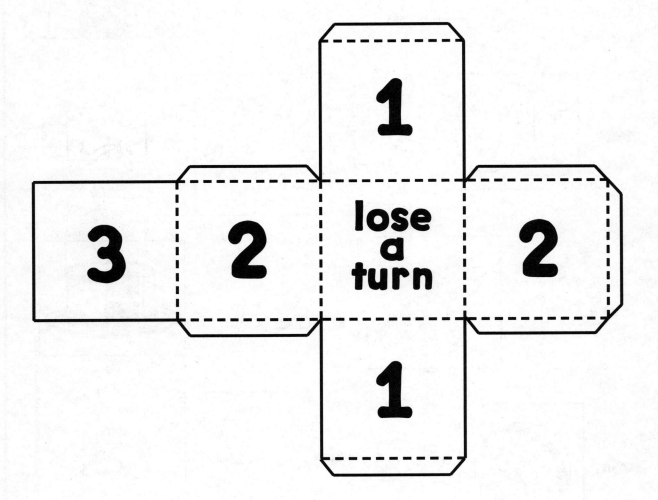

ACTIVITY 10: Picture Cards ....

SKILL: oddity task

Make copies of the picture cards on pages 28 and 29. Paste each picture on a note card and color or decorate as desired. Then display the following picture card set: *fan, feet, man, mop, six, soap.* Mix the cards, and have volunteers pick the two cards whose picture names begin with the same sound. When two cards are selected, say aloud the name of each picture and ask children to tell you what sound each begins with. Then have the children suggest other words that begin with the same sound as the two picture names.

The picture cards also can be used for these and other oddity tasks:

Picture Card Sets for Rhyme
- coat, boat, hat, cat, mop, top
- bat, hat, dog, log, goat, coat
- lock, sock, fan, pan, snake, cake

Picture Card Sets for Beginning Consonants
- fan, fish, leaf, lock, sock, sun
- bee, bus, gate, goat, ten, top
- can, coat, dog, duck, nest, nine

Picture Card Sets for Ending Consonants
- ball, wheel, can, sun, boat, feet
- kite, hat, ten, sun, mop, soap
- bus, glass, frog, pig, nine, man

Picture Card Sets for Medial Vowels
- soap, boat, leaf, feet, gate, cake
- bat, pan, top, sock, fish, pig
- lock, mop, goat, soap, man, hat

SUGGESTION BOX: Picture cards are particularly helpful for younger children. The visual cues allow them to think about the sounds in words without having to store a lot of information in their memory. For older children, however, you do not have to use picture cards. Instead, state the words in each oddity task. For example: *pig, big, hat.* Ask children to tell you the word that "does not belong," such as the word that does not rhyme.

For children having difficulties with the oddity tasks, use only two picture cards. Ask children if the two picture names begin with the same sound, end with the same sound, or rhyme, depending on what skill you are teaching. Then slowly increase the number of cards used, as appropriate.

Picture Cards

Picture Cards

ACTIVITY 11: Picky Puppet

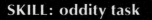

SKILL: oddity task

Distribute the set of picture cards on pages 28 and 29 evenly among the children. Each child should have at least two picture cards. Then use a classroom puppet or make a sock puppet for this activity. Explain to children that this puppet is a "sound puppet." This sound puppet only likes things whose names begin with a sound it chooses. For example, if the puppet likes licorice, it will also like other things whose names begin with /l/. Tell children that the sound puppet will name an object it likes. If they have any picture cards whose names also begin with the first sound in the object's name, the children are to hold up the cards. For example, if the puppet says, "I like tomatoes," the children holding the *ten*, *tie*, and *top* picture cards should hold up their cards. Have the puppet provide corrective feedback by reiterating the beginning sound of each card to check the children's responses. For example:

Puppet: I like marshmallows.
[One child holds up the *mop* picture card.]
Puppet: I see a mop.
M-m-mop. *Mop* begins with /m/, just like *mmmmmarshmallow.*

> Explicit phonemic awareness instruction has increased reading and spelling achievement among preschoolers, primary-grade children, and students with learning disabilities. (Ball & Blachman, 1991; Lundberg, Frost, & Petersen, 1988; Yopp, 1992)

ACTIVITY 12: Which Doesn't Belong?

SKILL: oddity task (practice page)

Which Doesn't Belong? can be used to assess children's abilities to do oddity tasks. The children will mark an X over the picture in each row that doesn't begin with the same sound as the other two pictures.

Use the *Which Doesn't Belong?* page as a template to make other oddity task pages. For example, use the following picture sets to make one page: 1: can, mop, cake; 2: sock, sun, pan; 3: feet, lock, leaf; 4: kite, ten, can; 5: gate, nest, nine.

> **SUGGESTION BOX:** In the early exercises, use only highly contrasting sounds such as /k/-/m/; /s/-/p/; /l/-/f/; /j/-/t/; and /w/-d/.

Which Doesn't Belong?

 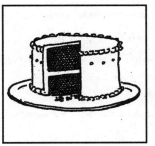  

ACTIVITY 13: How Does It End?

SKILL: oddity task (practice page)

How Does It End? can be used to assess children's abilities to do oddity tasks. The children will circle or color the picture whose name ends with the same sound as the picture in the box at the beginning of each row.

Use the *How Does It End?* page and the following picture sets as a template to make other pages:

1: <u>bat</u>, man, kite, top
2: <u>mop</u>, wheel, soap, dog
3: <u>lock</u>, duck, kite, fish
4: <u>ten</u>, kite, tie, sun
5: <u>box</u>, bat, six, nine

"Children who begin school with little phonemic awareness will have trouble acquiring the alphabetic principle which will, in turn, limit their ability to decode words." (Ball & Blachman, 1991)

How Does It End?

.... ACTIVITY 14: Sound Concentration

SKILLS: rhyme; beginning, medial, and ending sounds (game)

Materials:

concentration cards
(see page 35)

Setup

1. Make a copy of the concentration cards. Each card is
to be used with a different
game. Paste on the back of
each card one of the pictures
listed below for each game.
Use the pictures on pages 28
and 29 or cut out pictures from magazines.

• Use the following pictures for *Rhyme Time*: bat/hat, boat/coat, fan/man, clock/sock,
dog/frog, mop/top, snake/cake.

• Use the following pictures for *Start It Up!*: soap/sock, man/mop, leaf/lock, fish/fan,
nest/nine, ten/tie, pan/pig.

• Use the following pictures for *End It!*: bat/kite, box/six, dog/pig, duck/sock, can/sun,
soap/mop, ball/wheel.

• Use the following pictures for *What's in the Middle?*: boat/soap, cake/gate, leaf/feet, nine/kite,
cat/fan, top/sock, bus/sun.

2. Select one game to play. Spread out the cards for that game on a table. The pictures should
be facedown.

To Play *Rhyme Time*

1. In turn, each player turns over two cards and states aloud the name of each picture. If the two
cards contain a rhyming pair, such as *bat* and *hat*, the player gets to keep the cards. If the cards
do not rhyme, the player turns the cards over to their original position. The object of the game
is to remember where pictures are located so that pairs can be formed in future turns.

2. Each player continues in turn until all the pairs have been found. The player with the most
cards at the end of the game wins.

Start It Up!, *End It!*, and *What's in the Middle?* are played in the same way, with students finding
sound pairs.

Concentration Cards

Rhyme
Time

Start
It Up!

End
It!

What's
in the
Middle?

ACTIVITY 15: Put It Together

SKILL: oral blending

In *Put It Together*, you will say a word in parts. The children are to orally blend the word parts and say the word as a whole. To add to the playfulness of the activity, use a classroom puppet. Explain to the children that the puppet only likes to say whole words. You will say a word in parts and they are to guess what the puppet will say. The puppet can then provide corrective feedback and model blending, when necessary.

Sample:

Explain to children that you are going to say a word in parts. You want them to listen carefully, and then say the word as a whole. For example, if you say /m/ /a/ /n/, the children are to respond with *man*. Use these and other word parts:

- /m/ /a/ /p/ (map)
- /s/ /u/ /n/ (sun)
- /l/ /i/ /k/ (lick)
- /f/ /i/ /t/ (fit)
- /k/ /a/ /t/ (cat)

SUGGESTION BOX: Model for children how to blend sounds into words. For example, you might say, "I'm going to say a word very slowly, sound by sound. Then I'll say the word a bit faster. Finally, I'll say the word the way it is usually said. For example, if I hear the word parts /m/ /a/ /t/, I can blend them together like this: *mmmmmaaaaaat, mmaat, mat.*" Begin the modeling of blending with short CVC words (i.e., *sat, sun, map*) that start with continuous consonants such as *m, s, l, f,* and *r*. These sounds can be sustained without distortion and make it easier for children to discriminate and blend the sounds.

To help children visually note when you change from sound to sound as you blend the word, add movements. For example, you might move your hands from right to left as you change from sound to sound. Another technique is called "arm blending." Extend your left arm. Using your right hand, move your hand down your arm as you go from sound to sound in the word being blended. "Touch down" on the arm at each new sound. Have the children practice arm blending when they orally blend words. Left-handed children should extend their right arms.

Use the following sequence for *Put It Together* throughout the weeks of instruction:

Level 1: blend words syllable by syllable

> *Example:* sand . . . wich (sandwich)

Level 2: blend words by onset and rime

> *Example:* /m/ . . . ap (map)

> Note: A reverse of this level is to blend the first part of the word and then the final sound, such as ca . . . /t/.

Level 3: blend words phoneme by phoneme

> *Example:* /m/ /a/ /n/ (man)

ACTIVITY 16: Sound It Out ....

SKILL: oral blending

Write the song "Sound It Out" on chart paper. Sing the song to the tune of "If You're Happy and You Know It." At the end of the song, say a word in parts for children to orally blend. For example, /s/ . . . *at*. Then sing the song several times. At the end of each singing, point to a child to provide word parts for the class to blend.

Sound It Out
If you have a new word, sound it out.
If you have a new word, sound it out.
If you have a new word,
Then slowly say the word.
If you have a new word, sound it out.

"In order to benefit from formal reading instruction, children must have a certain level of phonemic awareness. Reading instruction, in turn, heightens their awareness of language. Thus, phonemic awareness is both a prerequisite for and a consequence of learning to read." (Yopp, 1992)

ACTIVITY 17: Old MacDonald Had a Box ....

SKILL: oral blending

Write the song "Old MacDonald Had a Box" on chart paper. Explain to children that this is a different version of the popular song "Old MacDonald Had a Farm." Track the print as you sing. Sing the song several times. During each singing, orally segment a different one-syllable word for children to orally blend. You might segment the word by onset and rime (/k/ . . . an) or phoneme by phoneme (/k/ /a/ /n/) depending on the children's instructional level. The following word parts can be used: /p/ . . . en, /s/ . . . ock, /m/ . . . p, /h/ . . . at, /t/ /o/ /k/, /t/ /o/ /p/, /f/ /a/ /n/, /b/ /a/ /t/.

Old MacDonald Had a Box
Old MacDonald had a box, E-I-E-I-O.
And in the box he had a /k/ . . . an, E-I-E-I-O
With a <u>can</u>, <u>can</u>, here
And a <u>can</u>, <u>can</u> there,
Here a <u>can</u>, there a <u>can</u>,
Everywhere a <u>can-can</u>.
Old MacDonald had a box, E-I-E-I-O.

As a variation, sing the original version of "Old MacDonald Had a Farm." Then have children change the E-I-E-I-O part by singing a rhyming counterpart, such as SE-SI-SE-SI-SO or ME-MI-ME-MI-MO.

ACTIVITY 18: Guess It!

SKILL: oral blending

The *Guess It!* game can be played in many ways. In this version of the game, you will orally segment the name of an animal. Children must guess the animal's identity. For example, you might tell children that you are thinking of the names of farm animals. The children must guess each animal's name.

Sample:
Teacher: I'm thinking of an animal. It's a /p/ . . . ig. What am I thinking of?
Children: A pig!

Continue with other categories such as zoo animals, classroom objects, numbers, colors, or household items.

As a variation, place the picture cards from pages 28 and 29 in a bag. Draw out one picture at a time. Tell children that you see a /k/. . . at, for example. Children are to orally blend the word parts to guess the picture name. Display the picture card for children to check their responses. Then invite children to be the "teacher" and segment the words for the class to guess. When children become skilled at segmenting and blending words by onset and rime, repeat the activity asking them to segment and blend the words phoneme by phoneme.

ACTIVITY 19: Draw It

SKILL: oral blending

Have children divide a sheet of paper into fourths. Then orally segment the name of an easily drawn object, such as a *hat*. Children will orally blend the word parts and then draw the picture in one section of the paper. In the early exercises, segment the words by onset and rime, such as /h/ . . . at. In later exercises segment the words phoneme by phoneme, such as /h/ /a/ /t/. Begin with two- or three-phoneme names (i.e., tie—/t/ /ī/; kite—/k/ /ī/ /t/) and progress to four-phoneme names (i.e., box—/b/ /o/ /k/ /s/).

ACTIVITY 20: Mystery Sentences ················

SKILL: oral blending

Read aloud sentences from a book, or sentences that you create. In each sentence choose one word to read in sound segments instead of as a whole word. The children must orally blend the word and then say it. Use sentences in which the children cannot guess the word based on context clues.

Sample:
Teacher: I gave it water when it was /h/ /o/ /t/.
When it was what?
Class: hot!

Use these and other sentences:
- I put a /p/ /e/ /n/ on the table. What did I put on the table? (a pen)
- The boy ran to the /b/ /u/ /s/. The boy ran to the what? (the bus)
- She is /f/ /ī/ /v/ years old. How old is she? (five years old)
- He found his red /s/ /o/ /k/. What did he find? (his red sock)
- I gave him my favorite /g/ /ā/ /m/. I gave him my favorite what? (game)

ACTIVITY 21: Name Game ·····················

SKILL: oral blending

When lining up children for recess or lunch, practice blending. Say a child's name in parts, such as /s/...am. The child whose name is segmented can get in line as the class blends the word parts to say their classmate's name.

········ ACTIVITY 22: What's the Sound?

Write the song "What's the Sound?" on chart paper. Sing the song to the tune "Old MacDonald Had a Farm." Track the print as you sing. Sing the song several times, encouraging children to join in. During later singings, replace the words *sad* and *silly* with the following: *mop* and *money*, *leaf* and *lucky*, or *ten* and *table*.

What's the Sound?
What's the sound that these words share?
Listen to these words.
<u>Sad</u> and <u>silly</u> are these two words.
Tell me what you've heard. (sssssss)
With a /s/, /s/ here, and a /s/, /s/ there,
Here a /s/, there a /s/, everywhere a /s/, /s/.
/s/ is the sound that these words share.
We can hear that sound!

SUGGESTION BOX: For children acquiring English, some sounds will be particularly difficult to auditorily discriminate or to pronounce. For example, in many languages consonant blends do not exist. In addition, some English sounds are often substituted, omitted, or confused with sounds in a child's primary language. For additional information on the challenges ESL children in your classroom might face, consult pages 131–151 in *The ESL Teacher's Book of Lists* by Jacqueline E. Kress (The Center for Applied Research in Education, 1993).

········ ACTIVITY 23: Can You Say?

Write the song "Can You Say?" on chart paper. Sing the song to the tune of "Happy Birthday." Track the print as you sing. Sing the song several times. Each time, replace the word *rabbit* with one of the following words: *mitten*, *happen*, *tablet*, *yellow*. Pause to provide children time to isolate the ending sound in each word. It might be necessary to emphasize the ending sound of each word for children having difficulties.

Can You Say?
Can you say the last sound?
Can you say the last sound?
It's the last sound in <u>rabbit</u>.
Can you say the last sound?

ACTIVITY 24: First Sound First ....

Ask children to listen to the following set of words: *sat, send, sick*. Point out that all these words start with the same sound. This sound is /s/. Tell children that you want them to listen carefully to each new set of words you say. They are to then tell you what the first sound is in these words. Finish the activity by having children state other words that begin with the sound.

SUGGESTION BOX: An early activity to begin working toward full segmentation of words is to have children segment just the first sound in a word. The children can then repeat, or reiterate, the sound. These iteration, or sound repetition, activities may be beneficial. Popular songs can be modified to include iterations. For example, when singing "Pop Goes the Weasel," have children sing "P-p-p-p-POP goes the weasel!" for the final line in the song.

Sample:

"Can you tell me what the first sound is in *fish, foot, fan*? That's right, it's /f/. What other words do you know that begin with /f/?"

Use these and other word sets: *man, mop, mitten; leaf, leg, lock; rabbit, run, rock;* and *ball, barn, big*.

ACTIVITY 25: Last Sound Last ....

Ask children to listen to the following set of words: *house, bus, mess*. Point out that all these words end with the same sound. This sound is /s/. Tell children that you want them to listen carefully to each set of words you say. They are to then tell you what the last sound is in these words. Finish the activity by having children state other words that end with the sound.

Sample:

"Can you tell me what the last sound is in *foot, bat, pet*? That's right, it's /t/. What other words do you know that end with /t/?"

Use these and other word sets: *fun, pen, moon; top, cup, soap; pig, leg, bug;* and *sack, rock, lick*.

ACTIVITY 26: Segmentation Cheer

SKILL: oral segmentation

Write "Segmentation Cheer" on chart paper and teach children the cheer. Change the words in the third line of the first stanza each time you say the cheer. The children are to segment this word sound by sound. You might wish to use these words in subsequent cheers: *soap, read, fish, lime, make, mop, ten, rat, pig, cat, dog, lip.*

SEGMENTATION CHEER

Listen to my cheer.
Then shout the sounds you hear.
Sun! Sun! Sun!
Let's take apart the word sun!

Give me the beginning sound.
    (Children respond with /s/.)
Give me the middle sound.
    (Children respond with /u/.)
Give me the ending sound.
    (Children respond with /n/.)

That's right!
/s/ /u/ n/—Sun! Sun! Sun!

"It is unlikely that children lacking phonemic awareness can benefit fully from phonics instruction since they do not understand what letters and spellings are supposed to represent." (Juel, Griffith, & Gough, 1986)

ACTIVITY 27: Big, Bigger, Biggest...............

SKILL: oral segmentation

Using the picture cards on pages 28 and 29, or pictures cut out from magazines, display two pictures. Ask children to count how many sounds they hear in each picture name. Then have children select the picture whose name has the most sounds. For example, if the two pictures are *pie* and *cat* the children would count two sounds for *pie* (/p/ /ī/) and three sounds for *cat*, (/k/ /a/ /t/). They would then choose *cat*, because it has more sounds. Continue with the following picture sets.

- tie (2), sun (3)
- leaf (3), bee (2)
- lock (3), clock (4)
- soap (3), snake (4)
- tie (2), six (4)

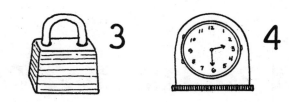

When children become skilled at this, increase the number of pictures to three.

ACTIVITY 28: Secret Sound ....

SKILL: oral segmentation

Explain to children that you are going to play a word game. You will say three words. You want them to listen closely and tell you what sound they hear that is the same in all the words. For example, if you say *teeth*, *bean*, and *feet*, children will respond with /ē/. Make sure the target sound is in the same position (initial, medial, or final) in all the words. Use the following word sets:

- sun, sick, send
- tell, top, tan
- ship, shark, shoe
- game, pain, late
- soap, road, note
- sight, ride, life
- team, game, home
- robe, cab, web
- doll, well, hill

ACTIVITY 29: I Spy

SKILL: oral segmentation

Display a favorite picture in a trade book, or have children look around the classroom. Explain to children that you are going to play a game called I Spy. To play, you will say something like "I spy with my little eye something that starts with /s/." You want them to guess the name of the object that begins with that sound.

As a variation, place an assortment of objects in a large bag. Select one object at a time and provide clues for children to guess the object's name. For example, for a pencil you might say, "I spy with my little eye something that begins with /p/. This is something you can write with. What is it?"

ACTIVITY 30: Listening Center

SKILL: oral segmentation

Place a tape recorder and a set of blocks in a listening center. On a tape, read aloud a list of ten words. Have children number a piece of paper from 1 to 10. Then, as they hear each word read, have them move one block for each sound they hear in the word. Have them count the number of blocks (the number of sounds in the word) and record that number on their paper. Provide the answers at the end of the tape for children to self-correct their papers. (You might wish to begin the tape by modeling a sample. For example, "*mat* has three sounds—/m/ /a/ /t/." Use the following set of ten words:

1. sat (/s/ /a/ /t/)
2. my (/m/ /ī/)
3. ice (/ī/ /s/)

4. ran (/r/ /a/ /n/)
5. pick (/p/ /i/ /k/)
6. leg (/l/ /e/ /g/)

7. take (/t/ /ā/ /k/)
8. soap (/s/ /ō/ /p/)
9. sell (/s/ /e/ /l/)

10. spell (/s/ /p/ /e/ /l/)

ACTIVITY 31: Buy It

SKILL: oral segmentation

Set up a mini-store in your classroom using school supplies or other small objects. Have children come to the store to "buy" one item. In order to buy an item, they must segment the item's name. For example, a child might say "I would like to buy a /p/ . . . en." If the child correctly segments the word (i.e., segments off the first sound), he or she can purchase the item.

ACTIVITY 32: One Potato ....

SKILL: oral segmentation

Teach the children the rhyme "One Potato." Then have small groups of children sit in a circle. As you say the rhyme, pass around an object such as a small beanbag. The child holding the beanbag at the end of the rhyme (on "more") must then state a word that begins with /p/, the first sound in *potato*. Then repeat the rhyme replacing the word *potato* with the suggested word. Continue until all children have had a chance to suggest a word. Next, change the word *potato* to *tomato*. In this version, the children will state words that begin with /t/. In subsequent days, choose other food names and sounds, such as *zucchini* (/z/) or *banana* (/b/).

One Potato
One potato, two potato,
Three potato, four;
Five potato, six potato,
Seven potato, more.

ACTIVITY 33: Where Is It? ....

SKILL: oral segmentation

Where Is It? will help children differentiate sound position in words. Distribute one counter to each child. Then have children draw three connected boxes on a sheet of paper (see sample on page 46). Tell children that you are going to say a list of words. All of the words contain /s/. Some words contain /s/ at the beginning, some in the middle, and some at the end. If children hear /s/ at the beginning of the word, they are to place the counter in the first box. If the hear /s/ in the middle, they are to place the counter in the center box. If they hear /s/ at the end, they are to place the counter in the last box. Use the following word list: *send, missing, sock, bus, less, passing, messy, safe.* In subsequent days, continue with other sounds and word lists. Use the following word lists:

- /p/—pack, mop, happy, pocket, hope, open, pudding, trap, pencil, keep
- /m/—man, moon, ham, summer, room, hammer, made, dream, lemon
- /d/—dog, duck, pad, pudding, middle, door, toad, read, puddle, dig

.........ACTIVITY 34: Sound Boxes

SKILL: oral segmentation

On the chalkboard, draw the following set of Sound Boxes.

SOUND BOXES

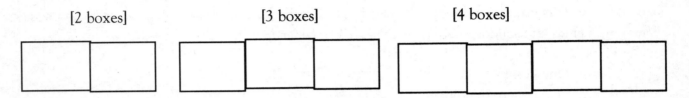

[2 boxes]   [3 boxes]   [4 boxes]

Say aloud a word. Children must segment the word, count the number of sounds, and then select the correct Sound Box that represents the word. For example, if you say the word *sit*, children will select the Sound Box containing three boxes—one for each sound in the word *sit* (/s/ /i/ /t/). To help children check their answers, model a "say-it and mark-it" procedure. You might say, "Watch me as I segment the word *sit*. Every time a hear a different sound, I will place a mark in one of the Sound Boxes." Extend the sounds in the word *sit* (*sssssssiiiiiiiit*) as you place one mark on each of three boxes. Continue with the following words:

egg (2)	mud (3)	fan (3)	nest (4)
ship (3)	pet (3)	ice (2)	it (2)
lip (3)	flip (4)	lit (3)	list (4)

> When children begin learning sound-spelling correspondences, have them write the spelling in each box for each sound in the word stated.

ACTIVITY 35: Count the Sounds ....

SKILL: oral segmentation

Distribute five counters and one copy of the Count the Sounds reproducible master on page 48 to each child. Explain to children that you are going to read aloud a word. They are going to count how many sounds they hear in the word, placing one counter on each box on the reproducible master. For example, if you say the word *sat*, children should place three counters on the reproducible master, one on each box. You might need to extend the sounds in each word for children to hear each discrete sound. For example, you might need to say *sssssaaaaat* for children having difficulty distinguishing the sounds in the word *sat*. You may also wish to add movements. For example, move your hands from right to left as you say the word, emphasizing when you change from one sound to another.

Have children segment each of the three related words in the vertical columns listed below before moving to the next set of words. Help them to understand that only one sound is different in each new word in the column. Ask them which sound in each new word is different.

> **SUGGESTION BOX:** Avoid segmenting words with blends until children can readily segment simple CVC words. When it is appropriate to segment words with blends, begin by using words that contrast by only one sound such as *lock/clock, sell/spell, tap/trap, net/nest.*

Use these and other words:

at	mop	run	in	cup
sat	map	sun	pin	cap
sit	tap	bun	pan	cat

> **As a variation** to the Elkonin segmentation boxes, have children do one of the following:
> • Tap out with a stick the number of sounds they hear in a word.
> • Walk in place or march the number of syllables or sounds they hear in a word.
> • Play on a musical instrument one note for each sound they hear. For example, beat on the drum one time for each sound in a word.

Count the Sounds

ACTIVITY 36: Graph It ....

Display the following picture cards from pages 28 and 29: tie, sun, mop, glass, bee, nest, fan, and leaf. Have children sort the cards according to the number of sounds each picture name contains. Then create a graph using the results of the sort.

2	3	4

ACTIVITY 37: How Many Sounds? ....

How Many Sounds? can be used to assess children's segmentation abilities. Have children look at the picture at the beginning of each row. The children will then orally segment the picture's name and color one box for each sound they hear in the word.

Use the How Many Sounds? page as a template to make other activity pages. Use the following pictures. Many can be found on pages 28 and 29.
- page 1: mop (3)*, pie (2), gate (3), sun (3)
- page 2: nine (3), sock (3), ice (2), egg (2)
- page 3: top (3), stop (4), bus (3), cake (3)
- page 4: lock (3), clock (4), net (3), nest (4)

* pertains to the number of sounds in the word

"Inefficiency in phonemic analysis (oral segmentation) and synthesis (oral blending) can interfere with learning and applying phonics principles." (Berninger, Thalberg, DeBruyn, & Smith, 1987)

How Many Sounds?

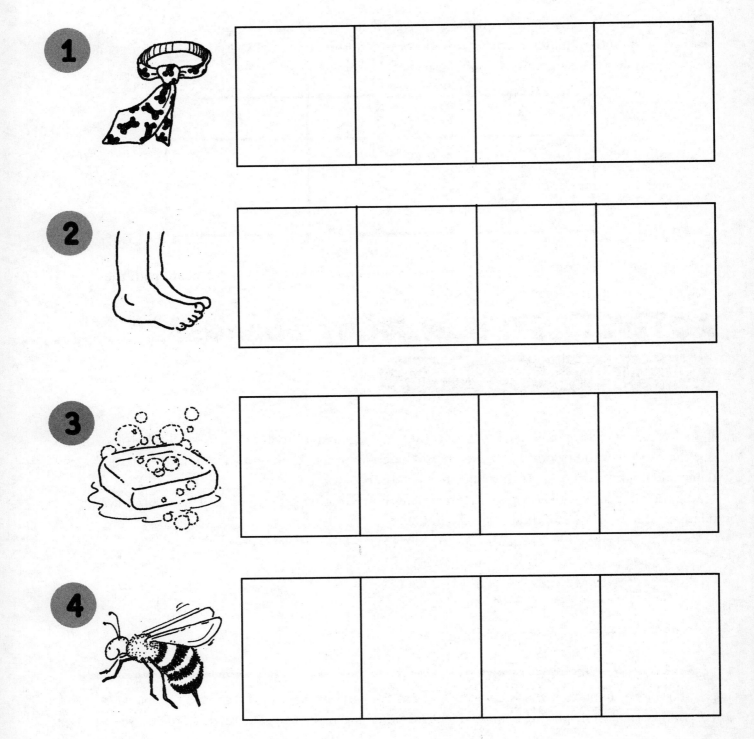

ACTIVITY 38: First Prize....

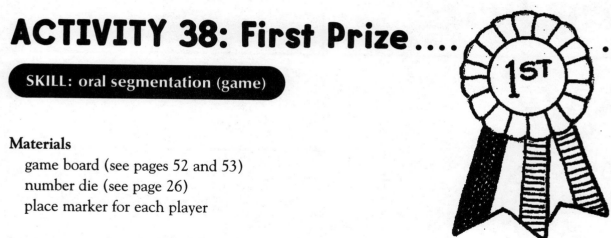

SKILL: oral segmentation (game)

Materials
    game board (see pages 52 and 53)
    number die (see page 26)
    place marker for each player

Setup
• Make a copy of the game board and number die. Construct the die by folding along the dotted lines and using tape to attach the die tabs to the die squares.

To Play
1. Each player chooses a place marker and puts it on START (the beginning of the search for first prize).

2. The first player throws the die and moves his or her marker along the game-board path the number of spaces on the die.

3. The player then states the name of the picture, repeating the first sound in the word. For example, if the player lands on the picture of the sun, he or she would say *s-s-sun*. If the player is unable to segment the first sound, he or she loses a turn.

4. Each player continues in turn. The first player to reach FINISH (the first-prize trophy) wins.

> "The combination—learning to separate and blend sounds while also learning how the alphabetic code represents sound—is a powerful union and the most likely to result in the greatest learning." (Fox, 1996)

First Prize

Activity 39: Initial Sound Switch

SKILL: phonemic manipulation (initial sound substitution)

Explain to children that you are going to play a word game. They are going to make new words by replacing the first sound in each word you say with /s/. For example, if you say the word *hand*, children are to say *sand*. Continue with these and other words:

hit	well	funny	bun
mad	bend	rat	rope

After children become skilled at substituting initial consonant sounds, repeat the same activity. This time have children substitute final consonant sounds (i.e., replace the last sound in *man* with /p/—*map*) and then medial vowel sounds (i.e., replace the middle sound in *ride* with /ō/—*rode*).

> **SUGGESTION BOX:** Model for children how to substitute a sound and make a new word. For example, explain to children that you are going to take a word and make new words using it. You might say "I can make a new word. I can take the /s/ off *sit,* put on a /p/, and I have a new word—*pit.* Can you take the /s/ off *sat* and put on a /m/ to make a new word? What is the new word?" (mat)

ACTIVITY 40: Row Your Boat.......................

SKILL: phonemic manipulation

Write the song "Row Your Boat" on chart paper. Have children sing the song a few times. Then tell children that you will sing it again, but this time you will change the line "Merrily, merrily, merrily, merrily" to "Serrily, serrily, serrily, serrily." To illustrate this, write the word *merrily* on the chalkboard, erase the letter *m*, and replace it with the letter *s*. This will help to illustrate that if you replace one sound in a word, you have a new word. Pronounce the nonsense word formed. Continue singing the song. Each time, change the first letter in the word *merrily* to create a new third line. You might choose to use the nonsense words *werrily*, *jerrily*, and *berrily*.

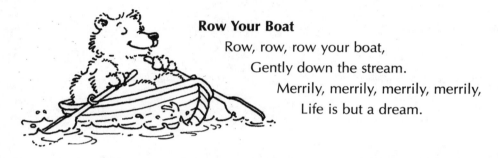

Row Your Boat
Row, row, row your boat,
Gently down the stream.
Merrily, merrily, merrily, merrily,
Life is but a dream.

You can do this same type of phonemic manipulation with other popular children's songs. These include the following:

• "I've Been Working on the Railroad": Substitute the initial sounds in "Fe-Fi-Fiddly-i-o" to make "Me-Mi-Middly-i-o" or "Se-Si-Siddly-i-o" and so on.

• "Happy Birthday": Substitute the initial sound throughout with /b/ to create lines such as "Bappy Birthday bo boo." In addition, you might substitute each syllable in the song with *la, lo, pa, bo,* or *ta.*

SUGGESTION BOX: The following books and songs contain examples of phonemic manipulation:

There's a Wocket in My Pocket by Dr. Seuss (Random House, 1989)
The Cow That Went Oink by Bernard Most (Harcourt Brace, 1990)
Don't Forget the Bacon by P. Hutchins (Morrow, 1976)
Zoomerang a Boomerang: Poems to Make Your Belly Laugh by Caroline Parry (Puffin Books, 1993)

"Apples and Bananas" from *One Light, One Sun* by Raffi (Crown Books, 1990)
"Willaby Wallaby Woo" from *Singable Songs for the Very Young* by Raffi (Troubadour Records Ltd., 1976)

ACTIVITY 41: Sound Switcheroo

SKILL: phonemic manipulation

Explain to children that you will say a word. You want them to listen carefully to the sounds in the word. You will then play switcheroo with one of these sounds. That is, you will change one sound in the word—the beginning, middle, or ending sound. You want them to tell you which sound was switched. For example, if you say *mat* and then *sat*, children should respond that /m/ was switched with /s/. Continue with the following word pairs:

- man/pan
- fan/fat
- run/sun
- hat/hot
- pick/pack

- ball/bell
- leaf/loaf
- pig/pin
- fish/dish
- gate/game

- tap/tape
- van/ran
- zip/lip
- cup/cap
- hot/hop

ACTIVITY 42: Consonant Riddles

SKILL: phonemic manipulation (initial sound substitution)

Explain to children that they are going to play a consonant riddle game. You will say a word. They are to think of a word that rhymes with your word and starts with a given sound. For example,

Teacher: What rhymes with *pat* and starts with /s/?
Children: sat

Continue with these and other riddles:
What rhymes with *hit* and starts with /s/? (sit)
What rhymes with *land* and starts with /h/? (hand)
What rhymes with *pick* and starts with /s/? (sick)
What rhymes with *fun* and starts with /r/? (run)

ACTIVITY 43: Sound of the Day ....

SKILL: phonemic manipulation (initial sound substitution)

Select a "Sound of the Day," such as /l/. Throughout the day, say children's names with that sound in place of the first sound. Peter will be called "Leter," Bonnie will be called "Lonnie," and Harry will be called "Larry." You may wish to take attendance this way and may want to encourage each child to experiment with saying his or her classmates' names with the sound of the day.

ACTIVITY 44: Picture Search ....

SKILL: phonemic manipulation (initial sound deletion)

Display a picture or a favorite page in a trade book. Explain that you will say the name of an object, animal, or person in the picture. However, you will say the name without its first sound. You want the children to guess the correct name. For example, if you see a picture of a dog, you would say *og*.

ACTIVITY 45: Sound Search ....

SKILL: phonemic manipulation

Say a three-phoneme word and the sound you are searching for. For example, say *feet* and ask for the first sound (/f/), or *fun* and ask for the middle sound (/u/). Use the following words and "Sound Search" questions:

- *leaf*: What's the middle sound? (/ē/)
- *sell*: What's the beginning sound? (/s/)
- *top*: What's the ending sound? (/pl/)
- *pan*: What's the middle sound? (/a/)

- *yes*: What's the beginning sound? (/y/)
- *wet*: What's the middle sound? (/e/)
- *make*: What's the middle sound? (/ā/)
- *rose*: What's the ending sound? (/z/)

ACTIVITY 46: Pick It Out

SKILL: phonemic manipulation (sound deletion)

The following exercises provide children with practice deleting sounds from words. State aloud a word and the word part or sound you want children to delete. For example, you might say "Say the word *sat* without the /s/." Children should respond by saying *at*. Point out to children that some of their responses will be nonsense or made-up words. Use the following words and clues:

word part
- say *sunshine* without the *sun*
- say *pancake* without the *pan*
- say *milkshake* without the *shake*
- say *doghouse* without the *house*

syllable
- say *cucumber* without the *cu*
- say *table* without the *ta*
- say *potato* without the *po*
- say *robot* without the *ro*

initial phoneme
- say *part* without the /p/
- say *sun* without the /s/
- say *back* without the /b/
- say *top* without the /t/

final phoneme
- say *meat* without the /t/
- say *ran* without the /n/
- say *mop* without the /p/
- say *take* without the /k/

initial phoneme in a blend
- say *stake* without the /s/
- say *smell* without the /s/
- say *green* without the /g/
- say *clock* without the /k/

final phoneme in a blend
- say *past* without the /t/
- say *nest* without the /t/
- say *bend* without the /d/
- say *belt* without the /t/

second consonant in an initial blend
- say *spell* without the /p/
- say *brake* without the /r/
- say *clap* without the /l/
- say *spoke* without the /p/

SUGGESTION BOX: These exercises are based on the research of J. Rosner. For additional information on these exercises, see *Helping Children Overcome Learning Difficulties* (Walker, 1979).

ACTIVITY 47: Color Cubes......................

SKILL: phonemic manipulation

Using the Color Cubes template on page 60 and colored paper, make the following set of cubes for each child: two red, two green, two blue, two yellow. Then display one cube; for example, a red cube. Explain to children that this cube stands for /i/. Have them add a cube to show *it*. Children should add a different-colored cube after the cube representing /i/ to show *it*. Then ask children to show you *hit*. Children should add a different-colored cube to the front of the two cubes representing *it*. Finally, ask children to show you *sit*. Children should replace the first cube in the three-cube series with a different-colored cube.

Continue with other words and sound additions, deletions, or substitutions. These exercises will help children focus on different sounds and their positions in words.

The following are examples of activities that can be done with these colored cubes:

- add a sound: "If this says /a/, show me *at*."
- delete a sound: "If this says *top,* show me *op*."
- change a consonant: "If this says *slip,* show me *snip*."
- change a vowel: "If this says *slip,* show me *slop*."
- change the order of sounds: "If this says *pats,* show me *past*."
- duplicate a sound already in the word: "If this says *art,* show me *tart*."

> **SUGGESTION BOX:** These exercises are based on the research of Lindamood and Lindamood (1969). For additional information, see *Auditory Discrimination in Depth* (DLM/Teaching Resources Corporation, 1984). Repeat these activities with letter tiles once children begin learning sound-spelling correspondences.

Color Cubes

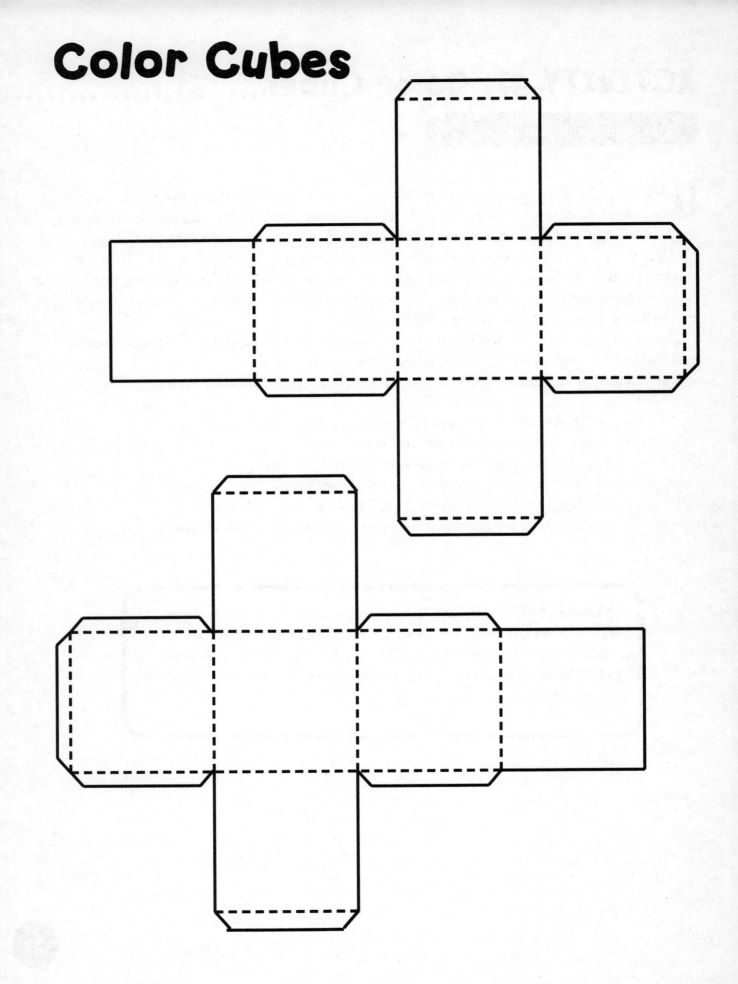

ACTIVITY 48: Sound-Spelling Match...........

SKILL: linking sounds to spellings

Once children's phonemic awareness skills begin to develop they will be ready for phonics instruction. It is important to show children how the phonemic awareness exercises you have been doing are related to reading and writing. To do this, use the following sound-spelling match exercises. For these exercises, each child will need a set of letter cards. Make copies of the letter cards on page 62. Distribute one set to each child. For these exercises you will focus on only a limited set of sounds. The purpose of these exercises is not to teach all sound-spelling correspondences, but to teach children the connection between the sounds they hear and reading and writing.

Step 1: teach the sound-spelling correspondences
- Using one letter card at a time, point out the sound that each letter stands for. For example, explain to children that the letter *s* stands for /s/, the sound heard at the beginning of the word *sock*. Have children suggest other words that begin with this sound. Once all the sounds and letters have been taught, say aloud one sound, and ask children to hold up the letter card that stands for the sound.

Step 2: review the sound-spelling correspondences
- Using the letter cards, review the sounds and letters taught. First, review the sound that each letter stands for. Then select one letter card, hold it up, and ask children to say aloud the sound that the letter stands for.

Step 3: build words
- Using the letter cards, spell the word *mat*. Review the sound that each letter stands for, then model for children how to blend the word *mat*. Replace the letter *m* in *mat* with the letter *s*. Review the sound that the letter *s* stands for, and model for children how to blend the new word formed. Continue replacing one letter in the word to form new words.

Step 4: replace sounds in words
- Using the letter cards, spell the word *sat*. Blend the word, or have a volunteer blend it aloud. Tell children that you are going to say a new word. This time you want them to replace one letter in the word *sat* to make the new word. For example, if you say the word *mat*, what letter must be replaced in the word *sat* to make *mat*? If necessary, point out that the letter *m* replaces the letter *s*. Continue with other sound substitutions.

Letter Cards

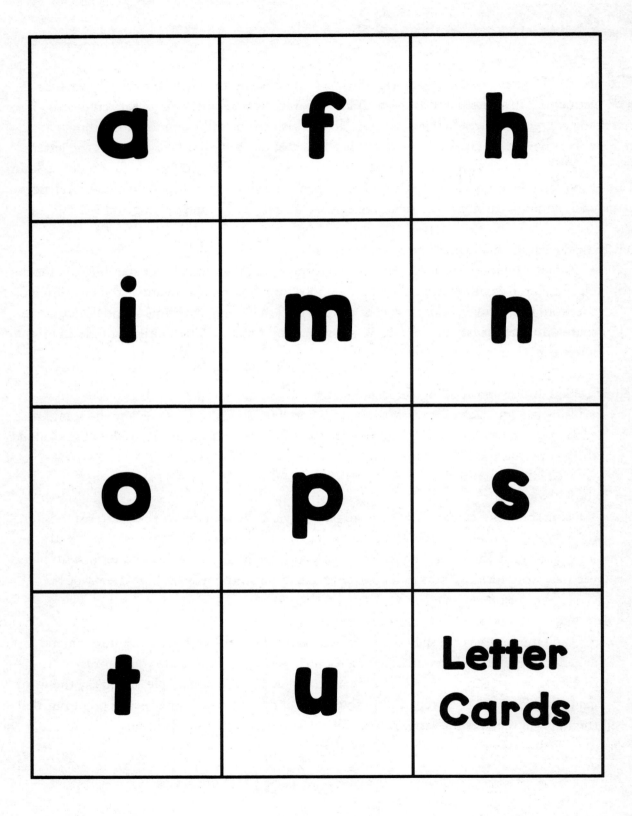

a	f	h
i	m	n
o	p	s
t	u	Letter Cards